Travel Through Time
Making Waves

Water Travel Past and Present

Jane Shuter

www.raintreepublishers.co.uk
Visit our website to find out more information about **Raintree** books.

To order:

☎ Phone 44 (0) 1865 888112
🗎 Send a fax to 44 (0) 1865 314091
💻 Visit the Raintree Bookshop at **www.raintreepublishers.co.uk** to browse our catalogue and order online.

First published in Great Britain by Raintree, Halley Court, Jordan Hill, Oxford OX2 8EJ, part of Harcourt Education.
Raintree is a registered trademark of Harcourt Education Ltd.

Editorial: Nick Hunter and Catherine Clarke
Design: Michelle Lisseter and bigtop
Picture Research: Maria Joannou and Kathryn Kollberg
Production: Jonathan Smith

Originated by Dot Gradations Ltd
Printed and bound in China by South China Printing Company

ISBN 1 844 43503 2
08 07 06 05 04
10 9 8 7 6 5 4 3 2 1

British Library Cataloguing in Publication Data
Shuter, Jane
Making Waves – water travel past and present. – (Travel Through Time)
387.5'09
A full catalogue record for this book is available from the British Library.

Acknowledgements
The publishers would like to thank the following for permission to reproduce photographs:
...; ATM Images pp. **21**, **27** (Pete ... Trafford); Bridgeman Art ... British Library p. **15**; British ... Corbis pp. **5**, **7** (Nick Wheeler), ... **0** (Museum of the City of New ... (Najlah Feanny), **29**; Hulton ... Illustrate London News Picture ... Mary Evans Picture Library pp. **14**, ... Maritime Museum p. **19**; National Museum of Denmark p. **11**; Photo Archiv (J. Leipe) p. **6**; Popperfoto p. **10**; Science and Society Picture Library p. **13**.

Cover photograph of a 1930s travel poster for Cunard Cruise ships reproduced with permission of Advertising Archives.

Every effort has been made to contact copyright holders of any material reproduced in this book. Any omissions will be rectified in subsequent printings if notice is given to the publishers.

The paper used to print this book comes from sustainable recsources.

Contents

Over the water 4

Early boats 6

Empire building 8

The Vikings 10

Trading and settling 12

Finding new lands 14

Canals 16

From sail to steam 18

Riverboats 20

Working steamers 22

Passenger steamships 24

Modern ships 26

Into the future 28

Find out for yourself 30

Glossary 31

Index 32

Any words appearing in bold, **like this**, are explained in the Glossary.

Over the water

People have always wanted to use seas and rivers to move around. Boats can get people further and faster than walking. They can also carry much more weight than a person or animal, and so can be used to carry heavy loads from place to place.

Seas and rivers were not used just for travel. Fish had always been an important food and boats help fishermen go further for more and different kinds of fish.

John White made this drawing of Native Americans fishing in 1584.

Homes on water

People have sometimes built their homes on islands in lakes or **lagoons**. They moved around by canoe. In the 1300s the Aztecs of Central America built two settlements on Lake Texcoco. The lake kept them safe from enemies.

HOW FAST?

The earliest sailors could only move as fast as they could paddle. Over 4000 years ago, an ancient Egyptian is said to have paddled a reed boat about 5 to 10 kilometres (3 to 6 miles) in an hour. In about 3100 BC people began to use sails . This made travel twice as fast, or more with a good wind. A modern sailing boat can reach speeds of about 48 kilometres (30 miles) per hour.

Venice, Italy, is a city built in a lagoon. Today most people move around the city on *vaporetti* – bus boats.

Early boots

Early peoples built simple boats that were small and light, with low sides. Light boats were easy to steer but also turned over easily in rough water. So early sailors stayed close to land, where the water was often calmer.

MAKING A BOAT

The earliest boats of all were probably made over 5000 years ago from natural materials that rotted and left nothing behind. In places with plenty of trees, people hollowed out logs for boats. In places with few trees, they used bundles of reeds tied together. From about 3000 BC people sewed animal skins together around a wooden boat frame, or filled them with air, so they would float.

This is a model of ancient Egyptian boats made from reeds.

Finding their way

Early sailors had no maps or **compasses** to help them **navigate** (find their way). They had to stay close to land. If they did this, they could watch the land for things they recognized, like a hill or a river going inland. As time passed, people made better boats. They added sails from about 3100 BC. These caught the wind to make the boats go faster. They used an oar at the back, to help steer.

The people of Iraq have never changed the **design** of their boats, because they work well and are cheap to build.

Empire building

The ancient Phoenicians, Romans and Greeks all lived around the Mediterranean Sea at different times from about 1000 BC to about AD 300. They built **empires** by taking over more and more land from other peoples. They needed two different kinds of boat for empire building.

Warships

Ships for fighting had to be fast and move about well. They had to carry a lot of men, who rowed the ship and fought at sea. Warships had rows of oars on both sides and not much space for anything else.

This is a Roman carving of trading ships coming into port.

Trading ships

Trading ships were bigger, heavier and slower. They had a lot of space for the **goods** and people they moved around the empires. Ships that sailed in the Atlantic Ocean were made from thick oak and had sails made from animal skins. They needed to be strong to cope with stormy weather.

PYTHIAS THE GREEK

Pythias the Greek sailed from the south of France (then in the Greek Empire) to Britain and on to Iceland 2300 years ago. He sailed on trading boats and in small light ships that stayed close to land. Compared to the Mediterranean Sea, he found the **currents** and waves of the Atlantic Ocean amazingly fierce.

This painting on an ancient Greek cup shows pirates, on the right, attacking a trading ship.

9

The Vikings

The Vikings lived in Scandinavia, in northern Europe. There were so many of them they needed more land and food. So the Vikings sailed off, first to **trade** with, or steal from, other lands and then to live there. They moved south across Europe, east into Russia and west to Iceland, Greenland and North America.

DIFFERENT BOATS

Viking longboats were used for fighting. They were long and sat higher in the water than earlier ships. This meant they could sail close to the shore and up shallow rivers to attack. They had no decks, just room for lots of rowers, who were also fighters. Viking trading ships were called knörrs.

Vikings used **compasses**, such as this one to help them sail out of sight of land.

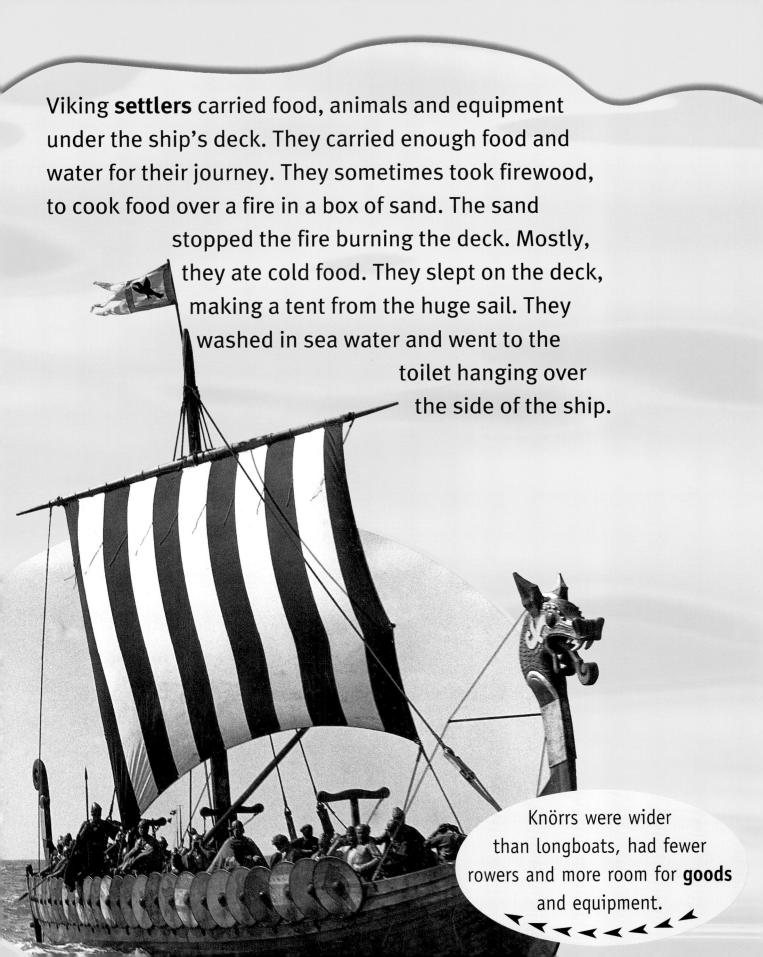

Viking **settlers** carried food, animals and equipment under the ship's deck. They carried enough food and water for their journey. They sometimes took firewood, to cook food over a fire in a box of sand. The sand stopped the fire burning the deck. Mostly, they ate cold food. They slept on the deck, making a tent from the huge sail. They washed in sea water and went to the toilet hanging over the side of the ship.

Knörrs were wider than longboats, had fewer rowers and more room for **goods** and equipment.

Trading and settling

From AD 1000, people built bigger ships that could carry far more **goods** and people. These ships were made to sail across the sea, out of sight of land. They had to cope with rough weather. People went exploring to find ways by sea instead of long and dangerous land journeys.

Not all change

People still made small fishing boats and bigger boats to sail close to land. The **design** of these boats stayed the same.

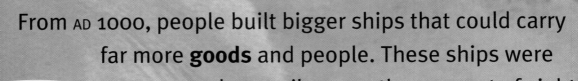

This painting from the 1400s shows small rowing boats (to travel short distances close to land) and larger sea-going boats.

Ships that went exploring stayed at sea for a long time. Sailors lived crowded together, with no privacy. They washed in sea water. The food and water they took with them often went bad before the end of their journey. They did not realize that they needed to eat fresh fruit and vegetables to stay healthy.

CROSSING THE SEAS

The earliest known use of these first **inventions** were:
- about 2000 BC, ancient Egypt, **rudder**, to steer at sea
- about 300 BC ancient Greece, astrolabe, to steer by the stars or Sun
- AD 1300 sea maps marked with **compass** directions.

The Chinese invented the first magnetic compass.

Finding new lands

By AD 1500 explorers from Europe had found many different lands. They made careful maps of their travels, which they kept secret. Each country hoped to find treasure. The Spanish who took over parts of South America were soon sending ships full of gold and silver back to Spain. The treasure attracted pirates, who captured the ships and stole everything on board.

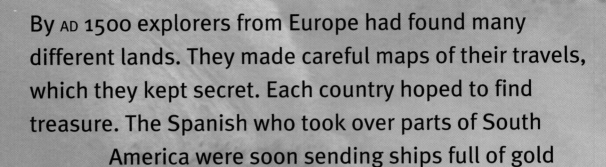

Francis Drake sailed around the world in the *Golden Hind*. This painting shows the great ship at sea.

As new lands were discovered, people **emigrated** there. Some of the first European **settlers** of North America travelled there on a ship called the *Mayflower*.

In this painting, these explorers are stranded because their ship has frozen in the icy waters and will not move.

GOING FURTHER

Explorers found new lands and, later, people went to live there:
- 1492 Christopher Columbus crossed the Atlantic to America
- 1519–22 one of five ships led by Ferdinand Magellan sails around the world. Of 234 men only 18 came back. Magellan died.
- 1577–80 Francis Drake sails around the world
- 1584 Sir Walter Raleigh sends settlers to Virginia.

Canals

Rivers and the sea do not always go where people want to go. So people began to dig their own waterways, called **canals**. When roads were just dirt and stone it was easier to carry heavy loads by water. The **Sumerians** built a canal nearly 160 kilometres (100 miles) long in 2400 BC.

An explosion of canals

The biggest problem with canals was going uphill. By AD 1700 people had solved this problem by building locks. Locks are boat-sized 'steps' with gates at either end. They are slowly filled with water or emptied, depending on whether a boat is going up or down the hill.

These boats are going into a lock near London, England, to go down.

Canals across narrow pieces of land can be useful short cuts. One famous 'short cut' canal is the Panama Canal (built 1907–14) joining the Atlantic and Pacific Oceans. After this canal was built, people no longer had to sail all the way around South America to get from one ocean to the other.

The Erie Canal in the USA was finished in 1825. It joined the Atlantic Ocean to the Great Lakes.

THE BEST WAY TO GO?

Canals were better and cheaper than roads for carrying heavy **goods**, such as coal. Canal travel was slow though, and canals were difficult and expensive to build. Roads began to improve and railways were **invented**. Heavy goods could now go more easily and cheaply by land, and people stopped building canals.

From sail to steam

In 1800, all ships were made from wood and sailed by wind power. Then, **steam power** was **invented**. In 1807 Robert Fulton launched the *Clermont*, the first reliable steamship. Sailing ships, especially 'clipper' ships, were faster and more reliable than early steamships.

Clipper ships had many more sails than early sailing ships, to use the wind as much as possible.

SAIL OR STEAM?

In the 1830s sailing ships took about 32 days to cross the Atlantic Ocean. If the winds were poor, it took longer. A steamship took 20 days, or less. Changes in design made steamships more and more **efficient**. By 1850 it took 14 days to cross the Atlantic, by 1900 it took just 5 days.

Early steamships had **design** problems. Their engines used a lot of coal and often broke down. Most had sails as well, to use if the engine failed or they ran out of coal. The first regular service across the Atlantic Ocean was run by four ships of the Cunard line. They carried mail and up to 63 passengers. The trip took fourteen days.

In 1838 the *Sirius* was the first ship to cross from Ireland to New York using just steam power. It took eighteen days, ten hours and ran out of coal. The sailors had to burn everything wooden to get there.

Riverboats

Riverboats had different problems from sea ships. Sailors did not lose sight of land, but had to worry about changes in the river. Some wide, slow rivers, like the Mississippi in the USA, had shifting banks of sandy **silt** that a boat could easily get stuck on.

By the 1880s Mississippi steamships were luxurious, with lots of food, drink and entertainment for the passengers.

Steamboats on the Mississippi

Paddle steamers were used on many US rivers from the 1830s. They provided a nicer choice to the dirty and dangerous journey by land. They also carried heavy loads, such as cotton, from big farms in the south.

Rivers, all over the world, were busy with lots of different boats, not just steamers. While paddle steamers were sailing the Mississippi, the River Yangtze in China was full of sampans, **barges** and sailing ships.

Some markets in Vietnam are held entirely on small boats.

SAMPANS

Sampans are small Chinese riverboats that have been in use for over a thousand years. They are small boats, with a covered part at the back to shelter people and **goods**. Modern sampans often have engines. Before this, they were rowed or pushed along with a long pole and steered by a long oar at the back.

Working steamers

By the 1890s almost all **cargo** ships were steamships. They were very reliable, unlike early steamships. They had more **efficient** engines that burned far less coal. The ship's main body, called the **hull**, was made from a new metal: steel. It was much stronger than wood.

The engine room of a steamship was hot, noisy and dusty.

BETTER STEAMSHIPS

These **inventions** helped steamships to go further, faster and more cheaply:

- 1836 propellers invented – stronger and more efficient than paddles
- 1840s iron hulls used – stronger than wooden ones
- 1870s steel hulls used – strong and lighter than iron ones
- 1884 turbine engine invented – used steam more efficiently to make a cheaper powerful engine.

Working steamships laid underwater telegraph cables across the Atlantic Ocean and to Australia. They carried mail and **goods** around the world. They got so big that small steamships, called tugs, had to 'tug' them up rivers and into ports.

Busy ports

The noisy docks of ports like London were crammed with ships and warehouses. Different goods unloaded in different parts of the docks. You could tell where you were by sniffing and smelling tea, spices or fruit!

In the 1880s special refrigerated ships were built to take meat around the world. They kept the meat cold and stopped it going bad.

Passenger steamships

The passenger ships of the 1850s carried animals to feed the passengers fresh meat along the way. Passengers had cabins to sleep in, but had to wash in sea water.

Big improvements

By the early 1900s, these ships, especially ocean liners crossing the Atlantic Ocean, were very luxurious. The *Titanic*, built in 1912, even had steam baths and its own telephone system.

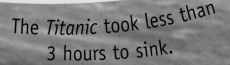

The *Titanic* took less than 3 hours to sink.

UNSINKABLE?

The *Titanic* was called 'unsinkable'. On its first crossing from Southampton to New York, in 1912, it hit an iceberg and sank. Over half of the 2340 passengers and crew on board died.

Disasters like the sinking of the *Titanic* made governments make stricter safety rules for passenger ships. Disasters did not stop people travelling on these ships. They were the only way to travel the world.

Only for the rich?

Prices for journeys depended on how many people you shared a cabin with and if you had meals. Poor people could travel 'steerage', crowded together in the most unpleasant parts of the ship with no meals or running water. This was the way many people **emigrated** from Europe to the USA in the early 1900s.

In the 1930s, posters such as this one made travel by ocean liner seem a grand adventure.

Modern ships

From 1945 onwards, ships have used modern technology to go further faster, and to be sailed by fewer sailors. Diesel engines, first used in ships in 1902, became much more **efficient** and took over from steam ones. Ships can carry far heavier loads than aeroplanes. **Cargo** ships now often carry the **goods** in large metal containers on the deck and below deck.

Tankers

There are also ships to carry just liquids, such as oil. They are called tankers. If these oil tankers have an accident the spilt oil causes terrible **pollution**.

These firefighters are trying to stop a blaze that has started after an oil spill.

New **inventions**, like **sonar** and **radar,** mean ships can travel in bad weather more easily. They use radios and computers to keep in touch with other ships and with people on shore.

This hovercraft is coming into land.

NEW WAYS OF TRAVELLING AT SEA

Regular passenger services of these inventions began to run:

- 1956 hydrofoils – used metal 'foils' underneath that act like water skis
- 1968 hovercraft – hovered just above the surface of the water on a cushion of air
- 1975 jetfoils – hydrofoils driven by a jet of water pushed out of the back.

Into the future

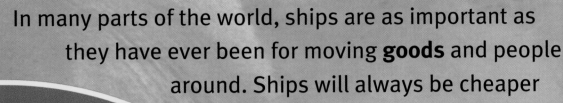

In many parts of the world, ships are as important as they have ever been for moving **goods** and people around. Ships will always be cheaper and more **efficient** in places were there is no rail transport, or where the roads are poor. With the **invention** of the aeroplane, however, people had found a new, faster way to travel.

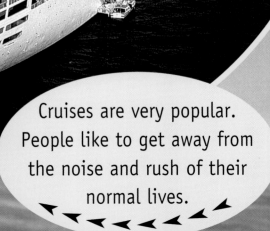

Cruises are very popular. People like to get away from the noise and rush of their normal lives.

Saving time

Planes save time. As soon as they were comfortable enough, more people used them to travel. Passenger ships are now mainly used for holiday cruises.

Ships will always be useful for transporting heavy goods and for fishing. The rising cost of oil means that ship **designers** need to look for a new fuel to power them. Transporting goods on oil-powered ships is getting too expensive.

Oil-powered ships also cause **pollution** if they have an accident. The Japanese are trying new and old fuels. One example is a magnet-driven ship, *Yamato I*.

YAMATO I

Magnets surround a water-filled pipe under *Yamato I*. Electricity is passed through it. This pushes the water out, hard enough to make the ship move.

Huge ships, such as this one, will still be used to carry heavy goods around the world.

Find out for yourself

You can find out more about the history of sea travel by talking to older people about how travel has changed during their lifetimes. Your local library will have books about this. They may have newspapers and magazine articles from the time, as well. You will find the answers to many of your questions in this book, but you can also use other books and the Internet.

Books to read
Speedy Machines: Boats, Vic Parker (Belitha Press, 1999)
Transport Around the World: Boats and Ships, Chris Oxlade (Heinemann Library 2001)
The Visual Dictionary of Ships and Sailing, Dorling Kindersley Publishing (Dorling Kindersley, 1991)

Using the Internet
Explore the Internet to find out more about sea travel. Websites can change, but if one of the links below no longer works, don't worry. Use a search engine, such as www.yahooligans.com or www.internet4kids.com, and type in keywords such as 'longboat', '**canal**', '*Titanic*' and '*Yamoto I*'.

Websites
http://www.bbc.co.uk/schools/vikings/travel/index.shtml
Find out more about Viking ships and sailors.
http://www.maryrose.org/lcity/index/htm
Meet the crew and find out what life was like on board the *Mary Rose*.

Glossary

barge boat with a wide, flat bottom, to go up shallow rivers and canals

canal waterway made by people

cargo things carried on a ship or other vehicle

compass object used to find your way

current movement of water in the sea in certain directions. Strong currents can make sea travel more difficult.

design to think of a way of making something to do a certain job

efficient work well

emigrate leave your own country to go and live in another one

empire all the lands controlled by one country

goods things that are made, bought and sold

hull frame of a ship including the bottom, sides and deck

invent make or discover something for the first time

lagoon sea water close to land partly cut off from the sea by a long strip of sand

navigate to find the way from one place to another

pollution causing damage to the natural world, making it dirty, messy and often dangerous for living things

radar when radio waves are bounced off objects to locate them

rudder oar at the back of a ship that moves to change the direction of the ship

settler person who moves from one place to live in another

silt fine mud, sand or soil that is moved around on the river bed as the river flows

sonar when sound waves are bounced off objects to locate them

steam power power made by burning coal under a sealed tank of water to create steam

Sumerian person or object coming from the ancient country of Sumer, which is now southern Iraq

trade buying and selling, or swapping, things

Index

astrolabe 13

barges 16, 21
bus boats 5

canals 16-17
canoes 5
cargo ships 4, 17, 20, 22, 23, 26, 29

clipper ships 18
compasses 7, 11, 13
cruises 28

diesel engines 26

early boats 5, 6–7
exploration 12, 13, 14–15

fishing boats 4, 12

hovercraft 27
hulls 22
hydrofoils 27

jetfoils 27

knörrs 10

locks 16
longboats 10

magnet-driven ships 29
modern ships 26–29

navigation 7, 11, 13

ocean liners 24, 25
oil-powered ships 26, 29

paddle steamers 20, 21
Panama Canal 17
passenger ships 19, 24–25, 28
pirates 9, 14
ports 23
propellers 22
Pythias the Greek 9

radar 27
reed boats 5, 6
refrigerated ships 23
riverboats 20–21
rudders 13

sailing boats and ships 5, 7, 8, 18, 21

sampans 21
sonar 27
steamships 18–19, 20, 22–25
steering 7, 13, 21

tankers 26
Titanic 24, 25
trading ships 9, 10
tugs 23
turbine engines 22

Vikings 10–11

warships 8

Titles in the *Travel Through Time* series include:

Hardback   1 844 43506 7

Hardback   1 844 43502 4

Hardback   1 844 43503 2

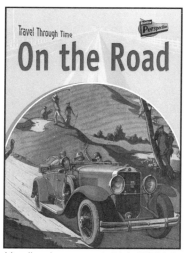

Hardback   1 844 43504 0

Hardback   1 844 43505 9

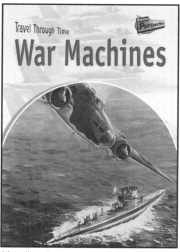

Hardback   1 844 43507 5

Find out about the other titles in this series on our website www.raintreepublishers.co.uk